Lift Me Up

You Can Do It!

Copyright © 2005 by Ron Kaufman
All rights reserved. The moral right of the author has been asserted.

Published by Ron Kaufman Pte Ltd - 10 9 8 7 6 5 4 3 2

Lift Me Up! - You Can Do It!
ISBN 981-05-2936-8 - 136 **pages**.

1. Motivation
2. Quotations
3. Self-Help
4. Ron Kaufman
5. Title

Cover and page layout by The Bonsey Design Partnership
Cover illustrations by Ngu Hie Ling
Set in Times and Arial fonts. Printed in Singapore.

Every effort has been made to credit the original author and make full acknowledgement of the source for each quotation in this text. However, if you know of any instance where the quotation or citation could be more accurate, please send a message to Ron@RonKaufman.com. Any corrections will gladly be included in future editions. Thank you.

Below each attributed quotation are **quips, quotes and anecdotes in bold text**. These additional notes are by Ron Kaufman (1956 –) who should be cited as the author in all future works.

Ron Kaufman, Lift Me Up!, Pick Me Up!, UP Your Service!, and a balloon with the word 'UP' are registered trademarks of Ron Kaufman Pte Ltd.

All rights reserved. No part of this book may be reproduced, stored, archived or transmitted in any form by mechanical or electronic means including information storage and retrieval systems without permission in writing from the publisher, except for the quotation of brief passages in book reviews.

Additional copies of this book are available at discount for promotional events, contests, awards and in-house training programs. For details and fast delivery, contact:

Ron Kaufman Pte Ltd
50 Bayshore Park #31-01
Aquamarine Tower
Singapore 469977

Tel: (+65) 6441-2760
Fax: (+65) 6444-8292
Ron@RonKaufman.com
www.RonKaufman.com

Contents

Your dreams and desires   *4*

Get into action   *30*

Believe in yourself   *68*

Never give up   *97*

Your dreams and desires

If men could regard the events of their own lives with more open minds, they would frequently discover that they did not really desire the things they failed to obtain.

André Maurois

Everything you *really* want is always within your reach.

You are what your deep driving desire is.

Brihadaranyaka
Upanishad

You achieve the most you are capable of, given all you do and all you believe.

Dreams do come true, if we only wish hard enough. You can have anything in life if you will sacrifice everything else for it.

J.M. Barrie

We trifle when we assign limits to our desires, since nature hath set none.

Christian Bovee

Do you want it enough? If you do, then go get it. If you don't, then don't complain.

Cutting down your dreams is pouring water on your inner fire.

One essential to success is that your desire be an all-obsessing one, your thoughts and aim be coordinated, and your energy be concentrated and applied without ceasing.

Claude Bristol

All through nature, you will find the same law: First the need, then the means.

Robert Collier

Give your true desires your full attention.

Want it, and you might find a way. Need it, and the way will find itself.

You can be anything you want to be, have anything you desire, accomplish anything you set out to accomplish – if you will hold to that desire with singleness of purpose.

Robert Collier

Make that which you want most the thing that matters most.

It is said that desire is a product of the will, but the converse is in fact true: will is a product of desire.

Denis Diderot

With intense desire comes a solid will.

Anything you really want, you can attain, if you really go after it.

Wayne Dyer

The significance of a man is not in what he attains, but rather what he longs to attain.

Kahlil Gibran

You already know you want it. Now, are you ready to chase it?

If you want to make a greater you, dare to dream of greater things.

One can never consent to creep when one feels an impulse to soar.

Helen Keller

Winning isn't everything, but wanting to win is.

Vince Lombardi

When you're driven to do more, anything less is not an option.

If you want to win, you've already begun the battle.

I believe that any single dream contains the essential message about our existence.

Frederick Perls

I always have to dream up there against the stars. If I don't dream I will make it, I won't even get close.

Henry Kaiser

Is a dream part of who we are, or do dreams make us who we are?

Big dreams are essential for big achievements.

For me, winning isn't something that happens suddenly on the field when the whistle blows and the crowds roar. Winning is something that builds physically and mentally every day that you train and every night that you dream.

Emmitt Smith

Dream as if you'll live forever. Live as if you'll die tomorrow.

James Dean

Don't work for your success, live for your success.

To make the most of your dreams, make the most of your days.

When you cease to dream you cease to live.

Malcolm Forbes

Act as if you have already achieved your goal and it is yours.

Robert Anthony

What would your life be without your dreams?

Your conviction is convincing.

We are what and where we are because we have first imagined it.

Donald Curtis

Imagination is everything. It is the preview of life's coming attractions.

Albert Einstein

Make it real in your mind. Let reality catch up.

Your imagination is the window to your future.

Imagination is not a talent of some people, but is the health of everyone.

Ralph Waldo Emerson

All the works of man have their origin in creative fantasy. What right have we then to depreciate imagination?

Carl Jung

Imagination is a gift given to everyone. Use yours to the fullest.

Everything fantastic was once a fantasy.

The opportunities of man are limited only by his imagination. But so few have imagination that there are ten thousand fiddlers to one composer.

Charles Kettering

Imagination decides everything.

Blaise Pascal

Don't just live the goals and dreams of others. Write your own script!

How far and wide can you see? Is it all that you can be?

Every great work, every great accomplishment, has been brought into manifestation through holding to the vision, and often just before the big achievement, comes apparent failure and discouragement.

Florence Shinn

Envisioning the end is enough to put the means in motion.

Dorothea Brande

A bump in the road just before the peak is where you need the determination to reach the top.

Imagine where you're going to be and you'll see the way to get there.

You have to think big to be big.

Claude Bristol

It takes someone with a vision of possibilities to attain new levels of experience. Someone with the courage to live their dreams.

Les Brown

The size of your dreams determines the size of your accomplishments.

Dream a dream that tests your courage.

Your goal should be out of reach but not out of sight.

Anita DeFrantz

Doing what you thought you could do is working. Doing more than you thought you could do is achieving.

Only he who can see the invisible can do the impossible.

Frank Gaines

When you can see what isn't yet there, you have the chance to make a difference.

Dreams can often become challenging, but challenges are what we live for.

Travis White

Your vision will become clear only when you can look into your own heart. Who looks outside, dreams; who looks inside, awakens.

Carl Jung

Let every challenge be a reminder that your life is worth living.

Look outside and you'll see what is there. Look inside and you'll see what can be.

It is a terrible thing to see and have no vision.

Helen Keller

If only we could pull out our brain and use only our eyes.

Pablo Picasso

Sight gives information. Vision offers transformation.

Your reasoned mind may argue against your cherished dreams. Be even more reasonable – ignore your mind0.

Throughout the centuries there were people who took first steps down new roads, armed with nothing but their own vision.

Ayn Rand

Create a vision and never let the environment, other people's beliefs or the limits of what has been done in the past shape your decisions. Ignore conventional wisdom.

Anthony Robbins

Move ahead. A new road can take you anywhere you want to go.

Conventional wisdom was once a bold vision. You can create a new one.

I was once asked if a big businessman ever reached his objective. I replied that if a man ever reached his objective he was not a big businessman.

Charles Schwab

The most important thing about a goal is having one.

Geoffrey Abert

Is the value in reaching your goals, or having great goals to reach for?

Even small goals have power to make you more than you are. Set one!

Man is a goal-seeking animal. His life only has meaning if he is reaching out and striving for his goals.

Aristotle

Choosing goals that are important to you is one of the most essential things you can do in order to live your dreams.

Les Brown

The more you strive, the more you are alive!

If you don't care enough, what you achieve will never be enough.

Objectives are not fate but direction. They are not commands but commitments. They do not determine the future but are the means to mobilize the resources and energies of business for the making the future.

Peter Drucker

Give me a stock clerk with a goal and I'll give you a man who will make history. Give me a man with no goals and I'll give you a stock clerk.

J.C. Penney

The future is yours to make. What are you creating?

Every goal gets you somewhere. No goals get you nowhere.

Setting goals is the first step in turning the invisible into the visible.

Anthony Robbins

A goal properly set is already on the way to its achievement.

Zig Ziglar

Every action begins with a decision to act.

Well begun is half done.

I visualize things in my mind before I do them. It's like having a mental workshop.

Jack Youngblood

The mind must see achievement of purpose before action is initiated.

Mack Douglas

Your imagination *is* a mental workshop. Use it.

If your mind can't see it, how can you believe it?

Ordinary people believe only in the possible. Extraordinary people visualize not what is possible or probable, but what is impossible. And by visualizing the impossible, they begin to see it as possible.

Cherie Carter-Scott

Begin to imagine what the desirable outcome would be like. Go over these mental pictures and delineate details and refinements. Play them over and over to yourself.

Maxwell Maltz

If you think something is impossible, you are not yet thinking.

When you imagine longer, you grow much stronger.

Great things are not done by impulse, but by a series of small things brought together.

Vincent van Gogh

If life were measured by accomplishments, most of us would die in infancy.

A.P. Gouthey

A string of small successes leads to great success.

It is never too early to achieve. It is also never too late.

Get into action

He who desires but does not act, breeds pestilence.

William Blake

Our goals can only be reached through the vehicle of a plan in which we must fervently believe and upon which we must vigorously act. There is no other route to success.

Stephen Brennan

A desire without action is demeaning.

You never know where the path will lead until you begin to walk.

It is easy to sit up and take notice. What is difficult is getting up and taking action.

Al Batt

The world can only be grasped by action, not by contemplation. The hand is the cutting edge of the mind.

Jacob Bronowski

Great people don't need to be pulled up – they've learned to push themselves up.

A thought is just a thought: Actions lead to changes.

You must take action now that will move you toward your goals. Develop a sense of urgency in your life.

Les Brown

Everything you want is out there waiting for you. Everything you want also wants you. But you have to take action to get it.

Jack Canfield

If it's truly 'now or never', will you do it now?

When you take action, what you want comes one step closer.

As I grow older, I pay less attention to what people say. I just watch what they do.

Andrew Carnegie

I never worry about action, but only inaction.

Winston Churchill

What you say tells us what you want to be. What you do shows us who you are.

Worry melts in the heat of action.

The superior man acts before he speaks, and afterwards speaks according to his action.

Confucius

First walk, then talk.

We keep moving forward, opening new doors, and doing new things, because we're curious. And curiosity keeps leading us down new paths.

Walt Disney

The only way to know what lies ahead is to find out.

Action may not always bring happiness; but there is no happiness without action.

Benjamin Disraeli

Do not be too timid and squeamish about your actions. All life is an experiment.

Ralph Waldo Emerson

You never know where an action will lead until you take it.

Good experiments get messy. Try anyway.

Your actions, and your actions alone, determine your worth.

Johann Fichte

Words may show a man's wit, but actions show his meaning.

Benjamin Franklin

Increasing what you do increases who you are.

Your actions speak louder than your words. What do your actions say about you?

Life is a series of steps. Things are done gradually. Once in a while there is a giant step, but most of the time we are taking small, seemingly insignificant steps on the stairway of life.

Ralph Ransom

A man is the sum of his actions; of what he has done, of what he can do, nothing else.

Mohandas Gandhi

The only way to reach the top is one step at a time. Keep stepping up!

Are you doing all you can do? Are you being all you can be?

Action is the foundation and key to all success.

Anthony Robbins

With no action, there is no result. With massive action, massive results.

Winners have simply formed the habit of doing things losers don't like to do.

Albert Gray

If you don't want to do something that would be good for you to do, that's reason enough for you to go ahead and do it.

Let us watch well our beginnings, and results will manage themselves.

Alexander Clark

Our business is not to see what lies dimly at a distance, but to do what lies clearly at hand.

Thomas Carlyle

You don't know where things will end. But they will always start at the beginning.

The only time you can act is now. Do what needs to be done.

In my beginning is my end.

T.S. Eliot

All this will not be finished in the first one hundred days. Nor will it be finished in the first thousand days, nor in the life of this administration, nor even perhaps in our lifetime on this planet. But let us begin.

John F. Kennedy

Making the best possible start leads to the best possible result.

When you can see what needs to be done, you must begin it, even if you will not see the end.

All great masters are chiefly distinguished by the power of adding a second, a third and perhaps a fourth step in a continuous line. Many a man has taken the first step. With every additional step you enhance immensely the value of your first.

Ralph Waldo Emerson

Successful people settle for nothing less than as many steps as it takes.

The quality of a person's life is in direct proportion to their commitment to excellence, regardless of their chosen field of endeavor.

Vince Lombardi

Excellence is not a choice of what to achieve but a choice of how to live.

If you want to achieve the most you can, take your eyes off reality and take a peak at possibility.

Shelley Wake

If you do not develop the hunger and courage to pursue your goal, you will lose your nerve and give up on your dream.

Les Brown

If you're too well-settled, you've probably settled.

Do you have hunger enough to want it? Do you have courage enough to seek it?

When a fantasy turns you on, you're obligated to life and nature to start doing it right away.

Stewart Brand

By going over the day in your imagination before you begin it, you can begin acting successfully at any moment.

Dorothea Brande

When an idea excites you, ignore how it seems and find out what it means.

Make the day successful in your imagination, and your imagination will help you make it real.

When you play it too safe, you're taking the biggest risk of your life.

Barbara Sher

Life leaps like a geyser for those who drill through the rock of inertia.

Alexis Carrel

Risk too little and you risk far too much.

Is human life about activity or inactivity?

You gotta be hungry!

Les Brown

When you're hungry, you will do what's necessary to eat. Get hungry for your goals.

It's easy to say 'no' when there's a deeper 'yes' burning inside.

Stephen Covey

Absolute commitment to your goals will save you from many unwanted distractions.

I have brought myself, by long meditation, to the conviction that a human being with a settled purpose must accomplish it, and that nothing can resist a will which will stake even existence upon its fulfillment.

Benjamin Disraeli

Genius begins great works; labor alone finishes them.

Joseph Joubert

Stake everything on succeeding and you leave the world no choice.

Beginning a new project is exciting. Completion is also exciting. But in between lies hard work. Are you ready to do it?

Nothing is more difficult, and therefore more precious, than to be able to decide.

Napoleon Bonaparte

Procrastination is the art of keeping up with yesterday.

Don Marquis

Every great decision is an act of trust and courage.

If you only do today what you should have done yesterday, you will rarely enjoy tomorrow.

Once you make a decision, the universe conspires to make it happen.

Ralph Waldo Emerson

Be bold and mighty forces will come to your aid.

Cathy Simon

When you choose to do something exceptional, the universe becomes your partner.

The powers of life far exceed what you and I will ever understand. Let them work magically beside you.

It doesn't matter on which side of the fence you get off sometimes. What matters is getting off. You cannot make progress without making decisions.

Jim Rohn

Decisiveness is a characteristic of high-performing men and women. Almost any decision is better than no decision at all.

Brian Tracy

Doing nothing gets you nowhere.

The quicker you make a decision, the quicker you can learn, correct and keep moving forward.

Desire is the key to motivation, but it's determination and commitment to the unrelenting pursuit of your goal that will enable you to attain the success you seek.

Mario Andretti

What this power is I cannot say; all I know is that it exists and it becomes available only when a man is in that state of mind in which he knows exactly what he wants and is fully determined not to quit until he finds it.

Alexander Graham Bell

Desire is the reason you want it. Action is the reason you get it.

When you know exactly what you want, add the fuel you need to get it.

A person who is gifted sees the essential point and leaves the rest as surplus.

Thomas Carlyle

Every year of my life I grow more convinced that it is wisest and best to fix our attention on the beautiful and the good, and dwell as little as possible on the evil and the false.

Richard Cecil

Does what matters the most matter most to you?

What you give your attention to will grow. That's why it's called 'paying attention'.

Concentration is the secret of strength in politics, in war, in trade; in short, in all the management of human affairs.

Ralph Waldo Emerson

Presence is more than just being there.

Malcolm Forbes

The results of concentration are no secret.

Whatever you are doing, give it everything you've got.

When a man knows he is to be hanged in a fortnight, it concentrates his mind wonderfully.

Samuel Johnson

Most people have no idea of the giant capacity we can immediately command when we focus all our resources on mastering a single area of our lives.

Anthony Robbins

To focus your mind, limit your time.

When you are focused, your power is focused.

Determine what specific goal you want to achieve. Then dedicate yourself to its attainment with unswerving singleness of purpose, the trenchant zeal of a crusader.

Paul Meyer

The man who can drive himself further once the effort gets painful is the man who will win.

Roger Bannister

Make the goal all yours and it will become you.

Pain is a reminder of what's worth striving for.

Hard work has made it easy. That is my secret. That is why I win.

Nadia Comaneci

There is no substitute for hard work.

Thomas Edison

The harder you work, the easier it becomes.

Time spent looking for the easy way is wasted.

If I am anything, I have made myself so by hard work.

Isaac Newton

When I was a young man, I observed that nine out of ten things I did were failures. I didn't want to be a failure, so I did ten times more work.

George Bernard Shaw

Easy work will never let you be all you could become.

You can't control every outcome. But you can control how many times you try.

I do not know anyone who has gotten to the top without hard work. that is the recipe. It will not always get you to the top, but it will get you pretty near.

Margaret Thatcher

When something is too easy, it's time to try something else.

Wanting something is not enough. You must hunger for it. Your motivation must be absolutely compelling to overcome the obstacles that will invariably come your way.

Les Brown

Obstacles are put in your way for two reasons: to assure you that what you are doing is worthwhile, and to assure the universe that you are the one worth doing it.

Experience shows that success is due less to ability than to zeal. The winner is he who gives himself to his work body and soul.

Charles Buxton

The discipline of writing something down is the first step toward making it happen.

Lee Iacocca

Enthusiasm isn't a skill to be learned, but a choice to be made.

When you write it down, you begin to make it real.

Whatever failures I have known, whatever errors I have committed, whatever follies I have witnessed in private and public life, have been the consequence of action without thought.

Bernard Baruch

In preparing for battle I have always found that plans are useless, but planning is indispensable.

Dwight D. Eisenhower

Think first, act smarter.

Planning for the future is a useful step to getting there.

By failing to prepare, you are preparing to fail.

Benjamin Franklin

Reduce your plan to writing. The moment you complete this, you will have definitely given concrete form to the intangible desire.

Napoleon Hill

Preparation is an investment in your future. Put plenty into it!

In your mind, ideas are only theory. In your notebook, ideas lunge toward reality.

He, who every morning plans the transactions of the day and follows that plan, carries a thread that will guide him through a labyrinth of the most busy life.

Victor Hugo

Planning what you have to do always helps to lead you through.

Waiting is a trap. There will always be reasons to wait. The truth is, there are only two things in life, reasons and results, and reasons simply don't count.

Robert Anthony

No reason is good enough.

Procrastination is one of the most common and deadliest of diseases and its toll on success and happiness is heavy.

Wayne Dyer

Don't wait. The time will never be just right.

Napoleon Hill

It is never too early to act. But it can quickly become too late.

You don't have enough time to wait for just the right time.

If you put off everything till you're sure of it, you'll never get anything done.

Norman Vincent Peale

Defer no time, delays have dangerous ends.

William Shakespeare

By the time you are sure of it, someone else has done it.

Time is always moving. Move with it.

If you don't fail now and again, it's a sign you're playing it safe.

Woody Allen

Most people live and die with their music still unplayed. They never dare to try.

Mary Kay Ash

Only through failures are lessons learned. Don't miss them.

Try and you might succeed. If you fail to try, you'll never know – and you'll never grow.

Play the game for more than you can afford to lose. Only then will you learn the game.

Winston Churchill

Watch the turtle. He only moves forward by sticking his neck out.

Lou Gerstner

When you limit what you put in, you limit what you get out.

If you want to get somewhere, take a risk.

Take calculated risks. This is quite different from being rash.

George Patton

Let a man who has to make his fortune in life remember this maxim: Attacking is the only secret. Dare and the world yields, or if it beats you sometimes, dare it again and you will succeed.

William Thackeray

Before you take the risk, know the risk. Protect yourself as much as you can – then jump.

A dream worth achieving is worth fighting for.

Believe in yourself

3

The challenge in life is to choose and operate through uplifting and fully empowering beliefs.

Michael Sky

Either you care or you don't.

Stanley Kubrick

Changing your world begins with changing yourself.

Care enough about yourself to believe in yourself.

The first requisite for success is the ability to apply your physical and mental energies to one problem incessantly without growing weary.

Thomas Edison

If you can't focus, you can't succeed.

Compared to what we ought to be, we are only half awake. Humans live far within their imagined limits. We are making use of only a small part of our physical and mental resources. We possess power of various sorts which we habitually fail to use.

William James

The person who believes he has limits, hasn't tested them.

Everyone's got it in him, if he'll only make up his mind and stick to it. None of us is born with a stop valve on his powers or with a set limit to his capacities. There's no limit to the expansion in each one of us.

Charles Schwab

No matter the level of your capability, you have more potential than you can ever fully develop in a lifetime.

James McCay

Limits are illusions. Once you reach them and test them, they disappear.

Don't leave without having tried!

I figured that if I said it enough, I would convince the world that I really was the greatest.

Muhammad Ali

It's the repetition of affirmations that leads to belief. And once that belief becomes a deep conviction, things begin to happen.

Claude Bristol

You can be the greatest, too. (First, convince yourself.)

Nothing can stop you from succeeding except deciding not to.

One comes to believe whatever one repeats to oneself sufficiently often, whether the statement be true or false, it comes to be the dominating thought in one's mind.

Robert Collier

Our subconscious minds have no sense of humor, play no jokes and cannot tell the difference between reality and imagined thought or image. What we continually think about eventually will manifest in our lives.

Sidney Madwed

You have the power to control your thoughts. Use that power to your advantage.

What you think about, comes about. So think about what you really want.

You will be a failure until you impress your subconscious with the conviction that you are a success.

Florence Shinn

Only one thing registers on the subconscious mind: repetitive application – practice. What you practice is what you manifest.

Grace Speare

Your subconscious mind is always listening. Keep saying good things.

To get something once, think it often.

There are no such things as idle thoughts. All your thinking works, either for good or bad.

Arnold Glasow

A positive attitude can make dreams come true – it did for me.

Zina Garrison

Every thought counts.

Positive people produce positive results.

The greatest discovery of my generation is that human beings can alter their lives by altering their attitudes of mind.

William James

Determination that just won't quit – that's what it takes.

A.J. Foyt

Your mind is yours and yours alone. What you make it will make you.

The moment you become unstoppable, the world will give you what you want.

A great attitude does much more than turn on the lights in our world; it seems to magically connect us to all sorts of serendipitous opportunities that were somehow absent before the change.

Earl Nightingale

Develop an attitude of gratitude, and give thanks for everything that happens to you, knowing that every step forward is a step toward achieving something bigger and better than your current situation.

Brian Tracy

A negative attitude blinds you to what is possible. A positive attitude opens your eyes.

If you wait until the end to give thanks, you won't appreciate how you got there.

I've never run into a guy who could win at the top level in anything today and didn't have the right attitude, didn't give it everything he had (at least while he was doing it), wasn't prepared and didn't have the whole program worked out.

Ted Turner

Do you have what it takes? Will you give all that it takes?

Some things have to be believed to be seen.

Ralph Hodgson

When everyone can see it, it's already there. When only you can see it, you're the one to put it there.

It doesn't matter how many say it cannot be done or how many people have tried it before; it's important to realize that whatever you're doing, it's your first attempt.

Wally Amos

Perpetual optimism is a force multiplier.

Colin Powell

And you might be the one who succeeds.

Let that force multiply in you.

Every person is the creation of himself, the image of his own thinking and believing. As individuals think and believe, so they are.

Claude Bristol

I always knew I was going to be rich. I don't think I ever doubted it for a minute.

Warren Buffett

The biggest choice you'll ever make is who you choose to be.

What you think really matters. What you know without thinking matters even more.

You are always a valuable, worthwhile human being – not because anybody says so, not because you're successful, not because you make a lot of money – but because you decide to believe it and for no other reason.

Wayne Dyer

Other people might know your worth, but you decide your value.

Belief creates the actual fact.

William James

Belief is the tool that makes an ideal real.

Only passions – great passions – can elevate the soul to great things.

Denis Diderot

Passion is a strong ladder. Start climbing.

If you are too scared to try or too scared to fail, then you are too scared to succeed.

Larry Ellison

Doubts? Throw them out.

Believe in yourself! Have faith in your abilities. Without a reasonable confidence in your own powers you cannot be successful or happy.

Norman Vincent Peale

You must win your own confidence first.

What we can or cannot do, what we consider possible or impossible, is rarely a function of our true capability. It is more likely a function of our beliefs about who we are.

Anthony Robbins

Challenge yourself to become more than you already think you are.

Faith is much better than belief. Belief is when someone else does the thinking.

R. Buckminster Fuller

If you think you can win, you can win. Faith is necessary for victory.

William Hazlitt

When you have faith, it comes from within.

Have faith in your own abilities. Life has already put its faith in you.

It's easy to have faith in yourself and have discipline when you're a winner, when you're Number One. What you've got to have is faith and discipline when you're not yet a winner.

Vince Lombardi

We would accomplish many more things if we did not think of them as impossible.

Chretien Malesherbes

If you are already a winner, you know it. If you are a winner-in-the-making, you must believe it.

Test the impossible to find out what is not.

There is nothing impossible to him who will try.

Alexander the Great

Impossible is a word only to be found in the dictionary of fools.

Napoleon Bonaparte

All improbable achievements were impossible before someone dared to try.

Respell 'impossible' – I-M-Possible.

Wilbur and Orville Wright flew through the smoke screen of impossibility.

Dorothea Brande

Most of the things worth doing in the world had been declared impossible before they were done.

Louis Brandeis

Impossible is a theory waiting to be disproved.

The difference between impossible and possible is someone's time and effort. Make it yours.

Those who dare are rare.

Richard Branson

All who have accomplished great things have had a great aim, have fixed their gaze on a goal which was high, one which sometimes seemed impossible.

Orison Marden

Difficulty is not a barrier to stop you, but a hurdle for you to leap.

The goal that seems impossible is the goal that's high enough.

Life has no limitations except the ones you make.

Les Brown

Live without boundaries.

Our aspirations are our possibilities.

Robert Browning

What you dare to dream is what you can achieve.

We all have possibilities we don't know about. We can do things we don't even dream we can do.

Dale Carnegie

The only way to discover the limits of the possible is to go beyond them into the impossible.

Arthur C. Clarke

What you are capable of isn't always visible. It's waiting to be discovered – by you.

Beyond the village, beyond the horizon, beyond the atmosphere, beyond the moon, beyond the stars. To move the limits, humans go beyond them.

When impossibility has been eliminated, whatever remains, no matter how improbable, is possible.

Arthur Conan Doyle

An important key to success is self-confidence. An important key to self-confidence is preparation.

Arthur Ashe

To learn what is possible, test what appears impossible.

Preparation is the soil, confidence is the seed, success is the fruit.

The history of the world is full of people who rose to leadership by sheer force of self-confidence, bravery and tenacity.

Mohandas Gandhi

You can do it, too.

Those who believe they are right often achieve something.

Aldous Huxley

Certainty paves the pathway to achievement.

Do not attempt to do a thing unless you are sure of yourself; but do not relinquish it simply because someone else is not sure of you.

Stewart White

Without self-confidence we are as babes in the cradle.

Virginia Woolf

You are the one who knows what you are capable of. You are the only one who can show what you're capable of.

To make more of yourself, think more of yourself.

Self-will so ardent and active that it will break a world to pieces to make a stool to sit on.

Richard Cecil

Nothing can withstand the power of the human will if it is willing to stake its very existence to the extent of its purpose.

Benjamin Disraeli

How much you believe determines much you can achieve.

There is no greater commitment than making what you want the reason for your being.

What you have to do and the way you have to do it is incredibly simple. Whether you are willing to do it, that's another matter.

Peter Drucker

Strength does not come from physical capacity. It comes from indomitable will.

Mohandas Gandhi

Success is not determined by what you have to do, but by whether you're willing to do it.

The strength of your mind has no limits.

Those who are firm in their will mold the world to themselves.

Johann Wolfgang von Goethe

People do not lack strength; they lack will.

Victor Hugo

How does the world shape you? How do you shape your world?

The strong may fail. But the determined will never fail because they never give up.

4

Never give up

No pressure, no diamonds.

Mary Case

When you can, you might.
When you must, you will.

To accuse others for one's own misfortunes is a sign of want of education. To accuse oneself shows that one's education has begun. To accuse neither oneself nor others shows that one's education is complete.

Epictetus

Blame no one. Conserve your energy. Keep trying!

Life is a series of experiences, each of which makes us bigger, even though sometimes it is hard to realize this. For the world was built to develop character, and we must learn that the setbacks and griefs which we endure help us in marching onward.

Henry Ford

Prosperity is a great teacher; adversity is greater. Possession pampers the mind; privation trains and strengthens it.

William Hazlitt

If you measure your experience only by your successes, you may miss the greater value.

Adversity has its own role in our lives. Great rewards often come after great struggles.

Every adversity, every failure, every heartache carries with it the seed of an equal or greater benefit.

Napoleon Hill

I used to hurt so badly that I'd ask, 'Why? What have I done to deserve any of this?' Now I feel I was preparing for the future.

Janet Jackson

The greatest problems inspire the greatest solutions.

Does the measure of difficulty tell you how hard it is, or how much better it can become?

Sometimes adversity is what you need to face in order to become successful.

Zig Ziglar

A time of hardship can inspire a lifetime of achievement.

When written in Chinese the word 'crisis' is composed of two characters – one represents danger and the other represents opportunity.

John F. Kennedy

When there is much to lose, there is much to be gained.

When things are bad, we take comfort in the thought that they could always get worse. And when they are, we find hope in the thought that things are so bad they have to get better.

Malcolm Forbes

Let obstacles become your great adventures.

Stanley Rhodes

It doesn't matter as much where you are now. What matters is where you are going.

A bad situation can inspire you to be your very best.

Difficulties increase the nearer we approach the goal.

Johann Wolfgang von Goethe

Life affords no higher pleasure than that of surmounting difficulties, passing from one step of success to another, forming new wishes and seeing them gratified.

Samuel Johnson

The more that stands in your way, the more there is to gain.

Difficulties are good reason for effort. Overcoming difficulties is good reason for joy.

Difficulty, my brethren, is the nurse of greatness – a harsh nurse, who roughly rocks her foster-children into strength and athletic proportion.

William C. Bryant

A convenient life is a small life.

Philip Hallstein

Do what is easy and it's done. Do what is difficult and you develop.

What's inconvenient makes you think and helps you grow.

You never will be the person you can be if pressure, tension and discipline are taken out of your life.

James Bilkey

Show me someone who has done something worthwhile, and I'll show you someone who has overcome adversity.

Lou Holtz

Being the best you can be isn't supposed to be easy.

The harder it is to get, the more it's worth the trouble.

We deem those happy who from the experience of life have learned to bear its ills without being overcome by them.

Carl Jung

Endurance is one of the most difficult disciplines, but it is to the one who endures that the final victory comes.

Buddha

You can't eliminate all the problems in life, but you can learn to stand up to them.

Endurance is worth the rewards. Keep going. Don't give up.

I know quite certainly that I myself have no special talent; curiosity, obsession and dogged endurance, combined with self-criticism have brought me to my ideas.

Albert Einstein

Talent is no substitute for perseverance. (But they do work well together.)

Failure is success if we learn from it.

Malcolm Forbes

When you fail to learn you have really failed.

My downfall raises me to infinite heights.

Napoleon Bonaparte

Life bows to an indomitable spirit.

We climb to heaven on the ruins of our cherished plans, finding only later that our failures were successes.

Amos Alcott

Success is built on a foundation of lessons learned from failure.

You may not realize it when it happens, but a kick in the teeth may be the best thing in the world for you.

Walt Disney

Or a kick in the behind.

Success consists of going from failure to failure without loss of enthusiasm.

Winston Churchill

Adversity is the seed of opportunity.

You will fail more often than you succeed. Your commitment to keep trying makes the difference.

Ron Kaufman

Every failure is a test. Pass them all.

The measure of a man is the way he bears up under misfortune.

Plutarch

Prosperity shows what people can do. Adversity reveals what they are made of.

Acceptance of what has happened is the first step to overcoming the consequences of any misfortune.

William James

Nothing stops the man who desires to achieve. Every obstacle is simply a course to develop his achievement muscle. It's a strengthening of his powers of accomplishment.

Eric Butterworth

Look back to find reasons. Look forward to find results.

Obstacles can strengthen or weaken you. It's your choice.

If you find a path with no obstacles, it probably doesn't lead anywhere worth going.

Frank Clark

Success is not measured by what you accomplish, but by the opposition you encounter and the courage with which you maintain your struggle against overwhelming odds.

Orison Marden

If it's too easy, it won't be worth it.

It's not only where you get to that matters, but how hard you work to get there.

A pessimist is one who makes difficulties of his opportunities and an optimist is one who makes opportunities of his difficulties.

Harry Truman

Our minds become magnetized with the dominating thoughts we hold in our minds. These magnets attract to us the forces, the people, the circumstances of life which harmonize with the nature of our dominating thoughts.

Napoleon Hill

Change your outlook and you change everything.

Take the controls of your mind and you take the controls of your life.

Our real blessings often appear to us in the shape of pains, losses and disappointments; but let us have patience and we soon shall see them in their proper figures.

Joseph Addison

The meaning of a failure often reveals itself only after you have reached success.

Never think that delays are denials. Hold on; Hold fast; Hold out. Patience is genius.

Georges-Louis LeClerc

**Denial means 'no'.
Delay means 'not yet'.**

It is by attempting to reach the top in a single leap that so much misery is produced in the world.

William Cobbett

Adopt the pace of nature; her secret is patience.

Ralph Waldo Emerson

There is a limit to how far you can leap. There is no limit to how many steps you can take.

The greatest things happen not because you demand them, but because you expect them and find the patience to wait for them.

He that can have patience can have what he will.

Benjamin Franklin

Every man must patiently bide his time. He must wait – not in listless idleness but in constant, steady, cheerful endeavors, always willing and fulfilling and accomplishing his tasks, that when the occasion comes he may be equal to the occasion.

Henry Wadsworth Longfellow

Chase and you might catch it. Wait and it may come to you.

Waiting is just the time it takes to be ready for what is to come.

Consider the hourglass; there is nothing to be accomplished by rattling or shaking; you have to wait patiently until the sand, grain by grain, has run from one funnel into the other.

Christian Morgenstern

You can have it all. You just can't have it all at one time.

Oprah Winfrey

The seed bears fruit in its own time. The fruit of your efforts will also come.

Success is not one day in your life, but every day of your life.

My philosophy of life is that when you make up your mind what you are going to make of your life, and then work hard toward that goal, you will never lose. Somehow you will win.

Ronald Reagan

It's no use saying, we are doing our best. You have got to succeed in doing what is necessary.

Winston Churchill

When you choose what to make of your life, you make the decision to win.

When you need to do more than you thought you could, you'll discover what you can do.

To get what you want, stop doing what isn't working.

Dennis Weaver

March on. Do not tarry. To go forward is to move toward perfection. March on, and fear not the thorns or the sharp stones on life's path.

Kahlil Gibran

When something doesn't work, don't wait for it to start working.

No matter what lies ahead, forward is the best direction.

Always seek out the seed of triumph in every adversity.

Og Mandino

I would never have amounted to anything were it not for adversity. I was forced to come up the hard way.

J.C. Penney

Ignorance is turning away from problems. Intelligence is looking at them until you see right through them.

The greatest lessons often come from the harshest failures.

People of mediocre ability sometimes achieve outstanding success because they don't know when to quit. Most men succeed because they are determined to.

George Allen

My greatest point is my persistence. I never give up in a match. However down I am, I fight until the last ball. My list of matches shows that I have turned a great many so-called irretrievable defeats into victories.

Bjorn Borg

The only time you stop your progress is when you choose to quit.

Nothing stops the person who never gives up.

Our greatest weakness lies in giving up. The most certain way to succeed is always to try just one more time.

Thomas Edison

I think and think for months and years. Ninety-nine times, the conclusion is false. The hundredth time I am right.

Albert Einstein

If you keep trying, the next time will be the one time that makes the difference. But you won't know which one it is until it happens. So just keep trying.

Each wrong answer is one step closer to the right one.

I'm proof against that word 'failure'. I've seen behind it. The only failure a man ought to fear is failure of cleaving to the purpose he sees to be best.

George Eliot

History has demonstrated that the most notable winners usually encountered heartbreaking obstacles before they triumphed. They won because they refused to become discouraged by their defeats.

B.C. Forbes

When you are connected to your purpose, you cannot fail.

Powerful people allow themselves to be tested, but never defeated.

We can do anything we want to if we stick to it long enough.

Helen Keller

I am not concerned that you have fallen – I am concerned that you rise.

Abraham Lincoln

If you stick to it long enough, you will get it.

How many times you fall down is unimportant. How many times you get back up is all-important.

This I know beyond any reasonable doubt: Regardless of what you are doing, if you pump long enough, hard enough and enthusiastically enough, sooner or later the effort will bring forth the reward.

Zig Ziglar

You can't expect continuous rewards but you must demand continuous effort.

We must free ourselves of the hope that the sea will ever rest. We must learn to sail in high winds.

Parsons Grant

Rough waters can power people forward.

Success is sweet; sweeter if long-delayed and gotten through many struggles and defeats.

Amos Alcott

Success is a journey not a destination. The doing is more important than the outcome. Not everyone can be Number One.

Arthur Ashe

Troubles along the way make the victory richer.

Success is not a point off in the distance. Success is what you're doing right here.

The toughest thing about being a success is that you've got to keep on being a success.

Irving Berlin

To guarantee success, act as if it were impossible to fail.

Dorothea Brande

Reaching the summit requires effort. Staying there requires more.

With no failure possible, every setback is just a setup for success.

You only have to do a very few things right in your life so long as you don't do too many things wrong.

Warren Buffett

Never lose sight of the fact that the most important yardstick of your success will be how you treat other people – your family, friends, coworkers, and even strangers you meet along the way.

Barbara Bush

Correct your mistakes. Let your successes run.

Your success is defined by those around you as much as by yourself.

In order to conquer, what we need is to dare, still to dare, and always to dare.

Georges Danton

Luck is tenacity of purpose.

Elbert Hubbard

When you have the courage to dare, you'll find the way to win.

Stay on purpose until good fortune finds you.

Every person who wins in any undertaking must be willing to cut all sources of retreat. Only by doing so can one be sure of maintaining that state of mind known as a burning desire to win – essential to success.

Napoleon Hill

Burn the boats when you reach the distant shore. Don't retreat – complete.

There is only one success – to be able to spend your life in your own way.

Christopher Morley

The only success you can create is your own.

There is no secret to success. It is the result of preparation, hard work, learning from failure.

Colin Powell

The way to success is to take massive, determined action.

Anthony Robbins

Time spent looking for shortcuts is time lost from creating success.

The more you seek to achieve, the more you must take action.

If you want to succeed you should strike out on new paths, rather than travel the worn paths of accepted success.

John D. Rockefeller

The most important single ingredient in the formula of success is knowing how to get along with people.

Theodore Roosevelt

Success must be created, not imitated.

Success can be yours, but you cannot create it alone.

The highest reward for a person's toil is not what they receive for their efforts, but what they become in the process.

John Ruskin

When you do the work required, you don't just achieve success. You also become successful.

Success is not the key to happiness. Happiness is the key to success. If you love what you are doing, you will be successful.

Albert Schweitzer

When you find joy in it, you'll find success in it.

To climb steep hills
requires a slow pace
at first.

William Shakespeare

We were born to
succeed, not to fail.

Henry David Thoreau

**Steady and slow will get
you where you want to go.**

**Success means living up
to who you are, not
struggling to become
something you are not.**

The key to success is to focus your conscious mind on things you desire, not things you fear.

Brian Tracy

If you want to be successful, find someone who has achieved the results you want, copy what they do and you'll achieve the same results.

Anthony Robbins

Desire catalyzes action. Fear paralyzes action.

Why do it all alone when there are so many who can guide you?

Thank you for choosing and sharing this book. With 512 inspiring quotes and uplifting notes this is my favorite:

> Let a man who has to make his fortune in life remember this maxim: Attacking is the only secret. Dare and the world yields, or if it beats you sometimes, dare it again and you will succeed.
> – William Thackeray

Which quote do you enjoy the most? Who can you share it with to help them succeed today?

Wishing you a world of success!

Ron Kaufman

To order more copies of the **Lift Me Up!**® books, visit your local bookstore or www.LiftMeUpBooks.com